SHAKESPEARE'S
LIGHT

OR
DESDEMONA'S
DREAM

Printed in the United States of America.

TJIKKO PUBLISHING
2501 N. Harwood Street, Suite 2001
Dallas, Texas 75201
tjikko.com

ISBN: 978-0-9909753-2-8
eISBN: 978-0-9909753-0-4

🌲 TJIKKO

For bearers of light who illuminate our world.

For bearers of light who illuminate our world.

PREFACE

Light in all its moods has always captivated me.

Light is life giving. Light illuminates the darkness, transforms our fears, and gives way to revelation, reason, and truth. For most of us, it also symbolizes warmth. My favorite childhood memories are infused with a certain sunlit quality—days riding a bicycle, playing with the dog, or paging through a book under the warm glow of a bare window.

In the house where I grew up, we had a library filled with books on Greek mythology, Roman architecture, and English renaissance literature. My father—who believed in a classical education—expected me to *read* those books. Whenever I had to miss school, protocol required calling each teacher to secure the day's assignments, plus—given the extra time—reading a selection from Shakespeare. Never mind the sweating, chills, and dizziness. Expect a quiz before dinner.

Given such jaundiced memories of days convalescing, it's a surprise, then, that this collection ever took form. I was working on a project about wisdom—specifically, how we learn to make better choices. Thinking an example or two of common dilemmas could illustrate certain points, I wondered, *Why not look at Shakespeare?* His plays abound with relatable predicaments: whether to choose love over family loyalty, mercy in favor of justice, or death to a life of suffering . . .

So, for the first time in years, I began rereading those plays
I'd tried to forget. And I was awestruck. For example, while
the interplay of light and dark is familiar in literature,
Shakespeare employed the contrast in remarkable ways—
to describe atmosphere, emotions, and even transcendent
states. Consider this scene from *Romeo and Juliet*, so widely
reproduced, one could be forgiven for skimming past
it. However, slowing to take in the words, who could be
unmoved?

> But soft, what light through yonder window breaks?
> It is the east, and Juliet is the sun.
> Arise, fair sun, and kill the envious moon,
> Who is already sick and pale with grief
> That thou, her maid, art far more fair than she . . .

For Romeo, Juliet is more than a source of beauty. She
represents life itself. She is his sun.

In total, there are nearly three hundred references to "light"
between *All's Well That Ends Well* and *A Winter's Tale*. What
follows is a collage abstracted from Shakespeare's words.
It can be read as a compilation of passages containing
the word light. Or, as I like to imagine, as glimpses of a
performance in progress, an invented narrative called
Desdemona's Dream.

Desdemona is, of course, the passionate beauty who elopes
with the title character of *Othello*. Her story is one of the

most tragic in all of Shakespeare. The casualty of a plot against her husband, she dies in his jealous hands. She would never know whether Othello realizes the magnitude of their loss. Or might she?

This is Desdemona's tale. The story begins at daybreak as Othello enters her darkened chamber. Looking on from above, she listens as he professes his love for her. Then, as morning turns to day, he recounts a fantastical story of a jilted prince, war, sacrifice, newfound love, marriage, and celebration. And as the tale draws to a close, day giving way to night, we return to the present. Alone with his beloved, Othello contemplates the consequences of his acts and what may be the greatest dilemma of all: Is a life separated from what you love worth living?

Perhaps in this retelling Desdemona finds peace in hearing his response.

Rugger Burke
May 2019

SHAKESPEARE'S
LIGHT

OR

DESDEMONA'S
DREAM

The grey-ey'd morn smiles on the frowning night,

Check'ring the Eastern clouds with streaks of light,

And fleckled darkness like a drunkard reels

From forth day's path and Titan's fiery wheels.

Now ere the sun advance his burning eye,

The day to cheer and night's dank dew to dry,

I must up-fill this osier cage of ours

With baleful weeds and precious-juiced flowers.

The earth that's nature's mother is her tomb;

What is her burying grave, that is her womb;

And from her womb children of divers kind

We sucking on her natural bosom find:

Many for many virtues excellent,

None but for some, and yet all different.

—*Romeo & Juliet*: 2.3.1–14

Enter Othello with a light

and Desdemona in her bed asleep.

—Othello: 5.2 (opening)

Titled goddess,

And worth it, with addition! But, fair soul,

In your fine frame hath love no quality?

If the quick fire of youth light not your mind,

You are no maiden, but a monument.

When you are dead, you should be such a one

As you are now; for you are cold and stern,

And now you should be as your mother was

When your sweet self was got.

—*All's Well That Ends Well*: 4.2.3–10

Take, O, take those lips away,

That so sweetly were forsworn,

And those eyes, the break of day,

Lights that do mislead the morn;

But my kisses bring again, bring again,

Seals of love, but seal'd in vain, seal'd in vain.

—*Measure for Measure*: 4.1.4–6

The brightness of her cheek would shame those stars,

As daylight doth a lamp; her eyes in heaven

Would through the airy region stream so bright

That birds would sing and think it were not night.

See how she leans her cheek upon her hand!

O that I were a glove upon that hand,

That I might touch that cheek!

—*Romeo & Juliet*: 2.2.19–25

Had I this cheek

To bathe my lips upon; this hand, whose touch

(Whose every touch) would force the feeler's soul

To th' oath of loyalty; this object, which

Takes prisoner the wild motion of mine eye,

Firing it only here; should I (damn'd then)

Slaver with lips as common as the stairs

That mount the Capitol; join gripes with hands

Made hard with hourly falsehood (falsehood, as

With labor); then by-peeping in an eye

Base and illustrious as the smoky light

That's fed with stinking tallow: it were fit

That all the plagues of hell should at one time

Encounter such revolt.

—*Cymbeline*: 1.6.98–110

Give me a taper! Call up all my people!

This accident is not unlike my dream,

Belief of it oppresses me already.

Light, I say, light!

—*Othello*: 1.1.135–138

Give me the light. Upon thy life I charge thee,

What e'er thou hearest or seest, stand all aloof,

And do not interrupt me in my course.

Why I descend into this bed of death

Is partly to behold my lady's face,

But chiefly to take thence from her dead finger

A precious ring—a ring that I must use

In dear employment—therefore hence be gone.

But if thou, jealous, dost return to pry

In what I farther shall intend to do,

By heaven, I will tear thee joint by joint,

And strew this hungry churchyard with thy limbs.

The time and my intents are savage-wild,

More fierce and more inexorable far

Than empty tigers or the roaring sea.

—*Romeo & Juliet*: 5.3.25–39

You are light into my hands,

where you are like to live.

—*Pericles*: 4.2.34

Methinks I am a prophet new inspir'd,

And thus expiring do foretell of him:

His rash fierce blaze of riot cannot last,

For violent fires soon burn out themselves;

Small show'rs last long, but sudden storms are short;

He tires betimes that spurs too fast betimes;

With eager feeding food doth choke the feeder;

Light vanity, insatiate cormorant,

Consuming means, soon preys upon itself.

—*King Richard II*: 2.1.31–39

Why, how now ho? From whence ariseth this?

Are we turn'd Turks, and to ourselves do that

Which heaven hath forbid the Ottomites?

For Christian shame, put by this barbarous brawl.

Holds his soul light; he dies upon his motion.

Silence that dreadful bell, it frights the isle

From her propriety. What is the matter, masters?

Honest Iago, that looks dead with grieving,

Speak: who began this? On thy love, I charge thee!

—*Othello*: 2.3.126–135

All to you. Lights, more lights!

—Timon of Athens: 1.2.182

That intemp'rate surfeit of her eye hath distemper'd

the other senses. They may return and settle again to

execute their preordain'd faculties,

but they are now in a most extravagant vagary.

This you must do: confine her to a place where the light

may rather seem to steal in than be permitted.

—*Two Noble Kinsmen*: 4.3.21

Beauty and honor in her are so mingled

That they have caught the King; and who knows yet

But from this lady may proceed a gem

To lighten all this isle?—I'll to the King,

And say I spoke with you.

—*Henry VIII*: 2.3.77–80

Perchance till after Theseus' wedding-day.

If you will patiently dance in our round,

And see our moonlight revels, go with us;

If not, shun me, and I will spare your haunts.

—*A Midsummer Night's Dream*: 2.1.139–142

Now then to recollection—was't not so?

A promise first of marriage—not a promise only,

for 'twas bound with surety of a thousand

oaths—and those not light ones neither.

Yet I remember too, those oaths could not prevail;

Th' unpractis'd maid trembled to meet my love:

By force alone I snatch'd th' imperfect joy,

Which now torments my memory. Not love,

But brutal violence prevail'd; to which

The time, and place, and opportunity,

Were accessaries most dishonorable.

Shame, shame upon it!

—*Double Falsehood*: 2.1.15–23

But that I love the gentle Desdemona,

I would not my unhoused free condition

Put into circumscription and confine

For the sea's worth.

But look, what lights come yond?

—*Othello*: 1.2.25–28

Yond light is not day-light, I know it, I;

It is some meteor that the sun exhal'd

To be to thee this night a torch-bearer

And light thee on thy way to Mantua.

Therefore stay yet, thou need'st not to be gone.

—*Romeo & Juliet*: 3.5.12–16

Enter at one door servants with lights,

Henriquez, Don Bernard, and Churchman.

At another, Ladies Attending on Leonora.

—*Double Falsehood*: 3.2.77

See, they are coming.

The waits plays; enter Lord Mayor,

so many Aldermen as may,

the Lady Mayoress in scarlet,

with other Ladies and Sir Thomas More's Daughters;

Servants carrying lighted torches by them.

—*Sir Thomas More*: 3.3.69

Yon king's to me like to my father's picture,

Which tells me in that glory once he was;

Had princes sit like stars about his throne,

And he the sun for them to reverence;

None that beheld him but, like lesser lights,

Did vail their crowns to his supremacy;

—*Pericles*: 2.3.37–42

Three glorious suns, each one a perfect sun,

Not separated with the racking clouds,

But sever'd in a pale clear-shining sky.

See, see, they join, embrace, and seem to kiss,

As if they vow'd some league inviolable.

Now are they but one lamp, one light, one sun.

In this the heaven figures some event.

—*Henry VI, Part 3*: 2.1.26–32

For his, it stuck upon him as the sun

In the grey vault of heaven, and by his light

Did all the chivalry of England move

To do brave acts. He was indeed the glass

Wherein the noble youth did dress themselves:

He had no legs that practic'd not his gait;

And speaking thick (which nature made his blemish)

Became the accents of the valiant;

For those that could speak low and tardily

Would turn their own perfection to abuse

To seem like him; so that in speech, in gait,

In diet, in affections of delight,

In military rules, humors of blood,

He was the mark and glass, copy and book,

That fashion'd others. And him, O wondrous him!

O miracle of men!

—*Henry IV, Part 2*: 2.3.18–33

Beyond repulse of wit or cure of art.

Now, in the sun alone it doth not lie,

With light to take light from a mortal eye;

—*Edward III*: 1.2.130–132

Yet looks he like a king! Behold, his eye,

As bright as is the eagle's, lightens forth

Controlling majesty. Alack, alack for woe,

That any harm should stain so fair a show!

—*King Richard II*: 3.3.68–71

Then, as my gift, and thine own acquisition

Worthily purchas'd, take my daughter.

But If thou dost break her virgin-knot before

All sanctimonious ceremonies may

With full and holy rite be minist'red,

No sweet aspersion shall the heavens let fall

To make this contract grow; but barren hate,

Sour-ey'd disdain, and discord shall bestrew

The union of your bed with weeds so loathly

That you shall hate it both.

Therefore take heed,

As Hymen's lamps shall light you.

—*The Tempest*: 4.1.13–23

No, yonder 'tis,

There where we see the lights.

—*Troilus & Cressida*: 5.1 (Ajax)

My Lord of Warwick, here is—praised be God for it!—

a most contagious treason come to light,

look you, as you shall desire in a summer's day.

Here is his Majesty.

—*Henry V*: 4.8.13

So,

They are well dispatch'd; now to my daughter's letter.

She tells me here, she'll wed the stranger knight,

Or never more to view nor day nor light.

'Tis well, mistress, your choice agrees with mine;

I like that well. Nay, how absolute she's in't,

Not minding whether I dislike or no!

Well, I do commend her choice,

And will no longer have it be delayed.

—*Pericles*: 2.5.15–22

Bethink you, father, for the difference

Is purchase of a heavy curse from Rome,

Or the light loss of England for a friend.

Forgo the easier.

—*King John*: 3.1.205–208

O good old man, how well in thee appears

The constant service of the antique world,

When service sweat for duty, not for meed!

Thou art not for the fashion of these times,

Where none will sweat but for promotion,

And having that do choke their service up

Even with the having. It is not so with thee.

But, poor old man, thou prun'st a rotten tree,

That cannot so much as a blossom yield

In lieu of all thy pains and husbandry.

But come thy ways, we'll go along together,

And ere we have thy youthful wages spent,

We'll light upon some settled low content.

—*As You Like It*: 2.3.68

Now all the plagues that in the pendulous air

Hang fated o'er men's faults light on thy daughters!

—*King Lear*: 3.4.47

Over thy wounds now do I prophesy

(Which like dumb mouths do ope their ruby lips

To beg the voice and utterance of my tongue)

A curse shall light upon the limbs of men;

Domestic fury and fierce civil strife

Shall cumber all the parts of Italy;

Blood and destruction shall be so in use,

And dreadful objects so familiar,

That mothers shall but smile when they behold

Their infants quartered with the hands of war;

All pity chok'd with custom of fell deeds;

And Caesar's spirit, ranging for revenge,

With Ate by his side come hot from hell,

Shall in these confines with a monarch's voice

Cry "Havoc!" and let slip the dogs of war,

That this foul deed shall smell above the earth

With carrion men, groaning for burial.

—*Julius Caesar*: 3.1.259–275

Know, thou sad man, I am not Tamora;

She is thy enemy, and I thy friend.

I am Revenge, sent from th' infernal kingdom

To ease the gnawing vulture of thy mind,

By working wreakful vengeance on thy foes.

Come down and welcome me to this world's light;

Confer with me of murder and of death.

There's not a hollow cave or lurking-place,

No vast obscurity or misty vale,

Where bloody murder or detested rape

Can couch for fear, but I will find them out,

And in their ears tell them my dreadful name,

Revenge, which makes the foul offender quake.

—*Titus Andronicus*: 5.2.28–40

Then thus I turn me from my country's light,

To dwell in solemn shades of endless night.

—*King Richard II*: 1.3.176–177

Discomfortable cousin, know'st thou not

That when the searching eye of heaven is hid

Behind the globe, that lights the lower world,

Then thieves and robbers range abroad unseen

In murders and in outrage boldly here,

But when from under this terrestrial ball

He fires the proud tops of the eastern pines

And darts his light through every guilty hole,

Then murders, treasons, and detested sins,

The cloak of night being pluck'd from off their backs,

Stand bare and naked, trembling at themselves?

—*King Richard II*: 3.2.36–46

The Prince of Cumberland! That is a step

On which I must fall down, or else o'erleap,

For in my way it lies. Stars, hide your fires,

Let not light see my black and deep desires;

The eye wink at the hand; yet let that be

Which the eye fears, when it is done, to see.

—*Macbeth*: 1.4.48–53

Nay, indeed if you had your eyes

you might fail of the knowing me;

it is a wise father that knows his own child.

Well, old man, I will tell you news of your son.

Give me your blessing; truth will come to light;

murder cannot be hid long; a man's son may,

but in the end truth will out.

—*The Merchant of Venice*: 2.2.20

Ha, good father,

Thou seest the heavens, as troubled with man's act,

Threatens his bloody stage. By th' clock 'tis day,

And yet dark night strangles the traveling lamp.

Is't night's predominance, or the day's shame,

That darkness does the face of earth entomb,

When living light should kiss it?

—*Macbeth*: 2.4.5–10

No, I'll be sworn, I make as good use of it

as many a man doth of a death's-head or a memento mori.

I never see thy face but I think upon hell-fire and Dives

that liv'd in purple; for there he is in his robes, burning,

burning. If thou wert any way given to virtue,

I would swear by thy face; my oath should be

"By this fire, that's God's angel." But thou art altogether

given over, and wert indeed, but for the light in thy face,

the son of utter darkness.

—*Henry IV, Part 1*: 3.3.7

More light and light,

more dark and dark our woes!

—*Romeo & Juliet*: 3.5.36

Where now his son's like a glow-worm in the night,

The which hath fire in darkness, none in light:

Whereby I see that Time's the king of men,

He's both their parent, and he is their grave,

And gives them what he will, not what they crave.

—*Pericles*: 2.3.43–47

As the moon does, by wanting light to give:

But then renew I could not, like the moon;

There were no suns to borrow of.

—*Timon of Athens*: 4.3.69–71

And so I was, which plainly signified

That I should snarl, and bite, and play the dog.

Then since the heavens have shap'd my body so,

Let hell make crook'd my mind to answer it.

I have no brother, I am like no brother;

And this word "love," which greybeards call divine,

Be resident in men like one another,

And not in me: I am myself alone.

Clarence, beware! Thou keep'st me from the light,

But I will sort a pitchy day for thee;

For I will buzz abroad such prophecies

That Edward shall be fearful of his life,

And then to purge his fear, I'll be thy death.

King Henry and the Prince his son are gone;

Clarence, thy turn is next, and then the rest,

Counting myself but bad till I be best.

—*Henry VI, Part 3*: 5.6.76–93

The night is dark,

light and spirits will become it well.

Heaven prosper our sport!

No man means evil but the devil,

and we shall know him by his horns.

Let's away; follow me.

Exeunt.

—*Merry Wives of Windsor*: 5.2.4

How now, my Lord of Worcester? 'Tis not well

That you and I should meet upon such terms

As now we meet. You have deceiv'd our trust,

And made us doff our easy robes of peace,

To crush our old limbs in ungentle steel.

This is not well, my lord, this is not well.

What say you to it? Will you again unknit

This churlish knot of all-abhorred war?

And move in that obedient orb again

Where you did give a fair and natural light,

And be no more an exhal'd meteor,

A prodigy of fear, and a portent

Of broached mischief to the unborn times?

—*Henry IV, Part 1*: 5.1.9–21

I will in Cassio's lodging lose this napkin,

And let him find it. Trifles light as air

Are to the jealous confirmations strong

As proofs of holy writ; this may do something.

The Moor already changes with my poison:

Dangerous conceits are in their natures poisons,

Which at the first are scarce found to distaste,

But with a little act upon the blood

Burn like the mines of sulphur.

—*Othello*: 3.3.322–330

Knew you not Pompey? Many a time and oft

Have you climb'd up to walls and battlements,

To tow'rs and windows, yea, to chimney-tops,

Your infants in your arms, and there have sate

The livelong day, with patient expectation,

To see great Pompey pass the streets of Rome;

And when you saw his chariot but appear,

Have you not made an universal shout,

That Tiber trembled underneath her banks

To hear the replication of your sounds

Made in her concave shores?

And do you now put on your best attire?

And do you now cull out a holiday?

And do you now strew flowers in his way,

That comes in triumph over Pompey's blood?

Be gone! Run to your houses, fall upon your knees,

Pray to the gods to intermit the plague

That needs must light on this ingratitude.

—*Julius Caesar*: 1.1.27–45

All the contagion of the south light on you,

You shames of Rome! You herd of—Biles and plagues

Plaster you o'er, that you may be abhorr'd

Farther than seen, and one infect another

Against the wind a mile! You souls of geese,

That bear the shapes of men, how have you run

From slaves that apes would beat! Pluto and hell!

—*Coriolanus*: 1.4.30–36

A plaguing mischief light on Charles and thee!

And may ye both be suddenly surpris'd

By bloody hands, in sleeping on your beds!

—*Henry VI, Part 1*: 5.3.40

Woe, woe for England, not a whit for me!

For I, too fond, might have prevented this.

Stanley did dream the boar did rase our helms,

And I did scorn it and disdain to fly.

Three times today my foot-cloth horse did scumble,

And started when he look'd upon the Tower,

As loath to bear me to the slaughter-house.

O now I need the priest that spake to me!

I now repent I told the pursuivant,

As too triumphing, how mine enemies

Today at Pomfret bloodily were butcher'd,

And I myself secure, in grace and favor.

O Margaret, Margaret, now thy heavy curse

Is lighted on poor Hastings' wretched head!

—*Richard III*: 3.4.80–93

Now, lords, for France; the enterprise whereof

Shall be to you as us, like glorious.

We doubt not of a fair and lucky war,

Since God so graciously hath brought to light

This dangerous treason lurking in our way

To hinder our beginnings. We doubt not now

But every rub is smoothed on our way.

Then forth, dear countrymen! Let us deliver

Our puissance into the hand of God,

Putting it straight in expedition.

Cheerly to sea! The signs of war advance!

No king of England, if not king of France!

—*Henry V*: 2.2.179–190

This battle fares like to the morning's war,

When dying clouds contend with growing light,

What time the shepherd, blowing of his nails,

Can neither call it perfect day nor night.

Now sways it this way, like a mighty sea

Forc'd by the tide to combat with the wind;

Now sways it that way, like the self-same sea

Forc'd to retire by fury of the wind.

—*Henry VI, Part 3*: 2.5.1–8

For what obscured light the heavens did grant

Did but convey unto our fearful minds

A doubtful warrant of immediate death,

Which though myself would gladly have embrac'd,

Yet the incessant weepings of my wife,

Weeping before for what she saw must come,

And piteous plainings of the pretty babes,

That mourn'd for fashion, ignorant what to fear,

Forc'd me to seek delays for them and me.

And this it was (for other means was none):

The sailors sought for safety by our boat,

And left the ship, then sinking-ripe, to us.

—*Comedy of Errors*: 1.1.66–77

But if the English blood be once but up,

As I perceive their hearts already full,

I fear me much, before their spleens be cold,

Some of these saucy aliens for their pride

Will pay for 't soundly, wheresoe'er it lights:

This tide of rage that with the eddy strives,

I fear me much, will drown too many lives.

—*Sir Thomas More*: 1.3.57–63

Dark needs no candles now, for dark is light.

—*Love's Labour's Lost*: 4.3.244

Why? Am I dead? Do I not breathe a man?

Ah, simple men, you know not what you swear!

Look, as I blow this feather from my face,

And as the air blows it to me again,

Obeying with my wind when I do blow,

And yielding to another when it blows,

Commanded always by the greater gust,

Such is the lightness of you common men.

But do not break your oaths, for of that sin

My mild entreaty shall not make you guilty.

Go where you will, the King shall be commanded;

And be you kings: command, and I'll obey.

—*Henry VI, Part 3*: 3.1.82–93

Who did strike out the light?

—*Macbeth*: 3.3.18

Though I did wish him dead,

I hate the murderer, love him murdered.

The guilt of conscience take thou for thy labor,

But neither my good word nor princely favor.

With Cain go wander thorough shades of night,

And never show thy head by day nor light.

Lords, I protest my soul is full of woe

That blood should sprinkle me to make me grow.

Come mourn with me for what I do lament,

And put on sullen black incontinent.

I'll make a voyage to the Holy Land,

To wash this blood off from my guilty hand.

—*King Richard II*: 5.6.39–50

And by our holy Sabbath have I sworn

To have the due and forfeit of my bond.

If you deny it, let the danger light

Upon your charter and your city's freedom!

You'll ask me why I rather choose to have

A weight of carrion flesh than to receive

Three thousand ducats. I'll not answer that;

But say it is my humor, is it answer'd?

—*The Merchant of Venice*: 4.1.36–46

Well, my lord, since you have given me leave to speak,

Freely will I speak. Antiochus you fear,

And justly too, I think, you fear the tyrant,

Who either by public war or private treason

Will take away your life.

Therefore, my lord, go travel for a while,

Till that his rage and anger be forgot,

Or till the Destinies do cut his thread of life.

Your rule direct to any; if to me,

Day serves not light more faithful than I'll be.

—*Pericles*: 1.2.101–110

Here burns my candle out; ay, here it dies,

Which whiles it lasted, gave King Henry light.

O Lancaster! I fear thy overthrow

More than my body's parting with my soul.

My love and fear glu'd many friends to thee,

And now I fall, thy tough commixtures melts,

Impairing Henry, strength'ning misproud York.

—*Henry VI, Part 3*: 2.6.1–7

If that it be the work of any hand?

We had a kind of light what would ensue.

It is the shameful work of Hubert's hand,

The practice and the purpose of the King;

From whose obedience I forbid my soul,

Kneeling before this ruin of sweet life,

And breathing to his breathless excellence

The incense of a vow, a holy vow,

Never to taste the pleasures of the world,

Never to be infected with delight,

Nor conversant with ease and idleness,

Till I have set a glory to this hand,

By giving it the worship of revenge.

—*King John*: 4.3.60–72

Away, you cutpurse rascal! You filthy bung, away!

By this wine, I'll thrust my knife in your moldy chaps,

and you play the saucy cuttle with me.

Away, you bottle-ale rascal!

You basket-hilt stale juggler, you!

Since when, I pray you, sir?

God's light, with two points on your shoulder?

Much!

—*Henry IV, Part* 2: 2.4.44

I take it up, and by that sword I swear

Which gently laid my knighthood on my shoulder,

I'll answer thee in any fair degree

Or chivalrous design of knightly trial;

And when I mount, alive may I not light,

If I be traitor or unjustly fight!

—*King Richard II*: 1.1.78–83

Upon mine honor, he shall never know

That I had any light from thee of this.

—*Two Gentlemen of Verona*: 3.1.48–49

And shall do so ever, though I took him at 's prayers.

Fare you well, my lord, and believe this of me:

there can be no kernel in this light nut;

the soul of this man is his clothes.

Trust him not in matter of heavy consequence;

I have kept of them tame, and know their natures.

Farewell, monsieur, I have spoken better of you

than you have or will to deserve at my hand,

but we must do good against evil.

—*All's Well That Ends Well*: 2.5.25–26

Up to the eastern tower,

Whose height commands as subject all the vale,

To see the battle. Hector, whose patience

Is as a virtue fix'd, today was mov'd:

He chid Andromache and struck his armorer,

And like as there were husbandry in war,

Before the sun rose he was harness'd light,

And to the field goes he; where every flower

Did as a prophet weep what it foresaw

In Hector's wrath.

—*Troilus & Cressida*: 1.2.4

It is, it is! Hie hence, be gone, away!

It is the lark that sings so out of tune,

Straining harsh discords and unpleasing sharps.

Some say the lark makes sweet division;

This doth not so, for she divideth us.

Some say the lark and loathed toad change eyes;

O now I would they had chang'd voices too,

Since arm from arm that voice doth us affray,

Hunting thee hence with hunt's-up to the day.

O now be gone, more light and light it grows.

—*Romeo & Juliet*: 3.5.26–35

Of hostile arms! Myself myself confound!

Heaven and fortune bar me happy hours!

Day, yield me not thy light, nor, night, thy rest!

Be opposite all planets of good luck

To my proceeding, if with dear heart's love,

Immaculate devotion, holy thoughts,

I tender not thy beauteous princely daughter!

In her consists my happiness and thine;

Without her, follows to myself and thee,

Herself, the land, and many a Christian soul,

Death, desolation, ruin, and decay.

It cannot be avoided but by this;

It will not be avoided but by this.

Therefore, dear mother—I must call you so—

Be the attorney of my love to her.

Plead what I will be, not what I have been;

Not my deserts, but what I will deserve.

Urge the necessity and state of times,

And be not peevish-fond in great designs.

—*Richard III*: 4.4.399–417

Give me some light. Away!

Lights, lights, lights!

—*Hamlet*: 3.2.190/191

There is but envy in that light which shows

The one the other. Darkness, which ever was

The dam of Horror, who does stand accurs'd

Of many mortal millions, may even now,

By casting her black mantle over both,

That neither could find other, get herself

Some part of a good name, and many a murder

Set off whereto she's guilty.

—*Two Noble Kinsmen*: 5.3.22–27

Nay, she is worse, she is the devil's dam,

and here she comes in the habit of a light wench;

and thereof comes that the wenches say,

"God damn me," that's as much to say,

"God make me a light wench."

It is written, they appear to men like angels of light,

light is an effect of fire, and fire will burn:

ergo, light wenches will burn.

Come not near her.

—*Comedy of Errors*: 4.3.30–34

How came she by that light?

Why, it stood by her.

She has light by her continually,

'tis her command.

—*Macbeth*: 5.1.8/9

It is the cause, it is the cause, my soul;

Let me not name it to you, you chaste stars,

It is the cause. Yet I'll not shed her blood,

Nor scar that whiter skin of hers than snow,

And smooth as monumental alabaster.

Yet she must die, else she'll betray more men.

Put out the light, and then put out the light:

If I quench thee, thou flaming minister,

I can again thy former light restore,

Should I repent me; but once put out thy light,

Thou cunning'st pattern of excelling nature,

I know not where is that Promethean heat

That can thy light relume.

When I have pluck'd thy rose,

I cannot give it vital growth again,

It needs must wither. I'll smell thee on the tree.

—*Othello*: 5.2.1–15

Let every word weigh heavy of her worth,

That he does weigh too light. My greatest grief,

Though little he do feel it, set down sharply.

Dispatch the most convenient messenger.

When haply he shall hear that she is gone,

He will return, and hope I may that she,

Hearing so much, will speed her foot again,

Led hither by pure love. Which of them both

Is dearest to me, I have no skill in sense

To make distinction. Provide this messenger.

My heart is heavy, and mine age is weak;

Grief would have tears, and sorrow bids me speak.

—*All's Well That Ends Well*: 3.4.32–43

Fond echo! Forego thy light strain,

And heedfully hear a lost maid;

Go, tell the false ear of the swain

How deeply his vows have betray'd.

Go, tell him, what sorrows I bear;

See, yet if his heart feel my woe:

'Tis now he must heal my despair,

Or death will make pity too slow.

—*Double Falsehood*: 4.2.16–23

O, I die, Horatio,

The potent poison quite o'er-crows my spirit.

I cannot live to hear the news from England,

But I do prophesy th' election lights

On Fortinbras, he has my dying voice.

So tell him, with th' occurrents more and less

Which have solicited—the rest is silence.

Dies.

—*Hamlet*: 5.2.269–275

Those that with cords, knives, drams, precipitance,

Weary of this world's light, have to themselves

Been death's most horrid agents, humane grace

Affords them dust and shadow.

—*Two Noble Kinsmen*: 1.1.143–145

He came with flowers to strew his lady's grave,

And bid me stand aloof, and so I did.

Anon comes one with light to ope the tomb,

And by and by my master drew on him,

And then I ran away to call the watch.

—*Romeo & Juliet*: 5.3.280–284

At length the sun, gazing upon the earth,

Dispers'd those vapors that offended us,

And by the benefit of his wished light

The seas wax'd calm, and we discovered

Two ships from far, making amain to us,

Of Corinth that, of Epidaurus this.

—*Comedy of Errors*: 1.1.88–93

Yonder comes a poet and a painter;

the plague of company light upon thee!

I will fear to catch it, and give way.

When I know not what else to do, I'll see thee again.

—*Timon of Athens*: 4.3.312

It appears, by his small light of discretion,

that he is in the wane; but yet in courtesy,

in all reason, we must stay the time.

—*A Midsummer Night's Dream*: 5.1.223

By this hand, I am.

Good fool, some ink, paper, and light;

and convey what I will set down to my lady.

It shall advantage thee more than ever

the bearing of letter did.

—*Twelfth Night*: 4.2.53

Let 'em not come too near. This maid,

For whom my sighs ride on the night's chill vapor,

Is born most humbly, though she be as fair

As nature's richest mould and skill can make her,

Mended with strong imagination.

But what of that? Th' obscureness of her birth

Cannot eclipse the lustre of her eyes,

Which make her all one light.

—Strike up, my masters;

But touch the strings with a religious softness;

Teach sound to languish through the night's dull ear,

'Till melancholy start from her lazy couch,

And carelessness grow convert to attention.

—*Double Falsehood*: 1.3.3–14

And yonder shines Aurora's harbinger,

At whose approach, ghosts, wand'ring here and there,

Troop home to churchyards. Damned spirits all,

That in crossways and floods have burial,

Already to their wormy beds are gone.

For fear lest day should look their shames upon,

They willfully themselves exile from light,

And must for aye consort with black-brow'd Night

—*A Midsummer Night's Dream*: 3.2.380–387

How came

His practices to light?

—*Henry VIII*: 3.2.27

Many a morning hath he there been seen,

With tears augmenting the fresh morning's dew,

Adding to clouds more clouds with his deep sighs,

But all so soon as the all-cheering sun

Should in the farthest east begin to draw

The shady curtains from Aurora's bed,

Away from light steals home my heavy son,

And private in his chamber pens himself,

Shuts up his windows, locks fair daylight out,

And makes himself an artificial night.

Black and portendous must this humor prove,

Unless good counsel may the cause remove.

—*Romeo & Juliet*: 1.1.108–119

What's your dark meaning, mouse,

of this light word?

A light condition in a beauty dark.

—*Love's Labour's Lost*: 5.2.19/20

Come, come; we'll couch i' th' castle-ditch
till we see the light of our fairies.

—*Merry Wives of Windsor*: 5.2.1

No, by this heavenly light!

Nor I neither by this heavenly light;

I might do't as well i' th' dark.

      —*Othello*: 4.3.63–64

O, train me not, sweet mermaid, with thy note,

To drown me in thy sister's flood of tears.

Sing, siren, for thyself, and I will dote;

Spread o'er the silver waves thy golden hairs,

And as a bed I'll take them, and there lie,

And in that glorious supposition think

He gains by death that hath such means to die:

Let Love, being light, be drowned if she sink!

—*Comedy of Errors*: 3.2.45–52

So sweet a kiss the golden sun gives not

To those fresh morning drops upon the rose,

As thy eye-beams, when their fresh rays have smote

The night of dew that on my cheeks down flows;

Nor shines the silver moon one half so bright

Through the transparent bosom of the deep,

As doth thy face through tears of mine give light.

Thou shin'st in every tear that I do weep,

No drop but as a coach doth carry thee;

So ridest thou triumphing in my woe.

Do but behold the tears that swell in me,

And they thy glory through my grief will show.

But do not love thyself, then thou wilt keep

My tears for glasses, and still make me weep.

O queen of queens, how far dost thou excel

No thought can think, nor tongue of mortal tell.

How shall she know my griefs? I'll drop the paper.

Sweet leaves, shade folly.

—*Love's Labour's Lost*: 4.3.4–21

He made her melancholy, sad, and heavy,

And so she died. Had she been light, like you,

Of such a merry, nimble, stirring spirit,

She might 'a' been a grandam ere she died.

—*Love's Labour's Lost*: 5.2.14–18

For my part, the sea cannot drown me;

I swam, ere I could recover the shore,

five and thirty leagues off and on.

By this light, thou shalt be my lieutenant,

monster, or my standard.

—*The Tempest*: 3.2.5

For here two day stars that mine eyes would see

More than the sun steals mine own light from me,

Contemplative desire, desire to be.

—*Edward 3*: 1.2.133–137

Because Love is blind.

O that you had mine eyes,

or your own eyes had the lights

they were wont to have when you

chid at Sir Proteus for going ungarter'd!

—*Two Gentlemen of Verona*: 2.1.41

Well; it shall be so. But there is two hard things:

that is, to bring the moonlight into a chamber;

for you know, Pyramus and Thisbe meet by

moonlight.

—*A Midsummer Night's Dream*: 3.1.16

But soft, what light through yonder window breaks?

It is the east, and Juliet is the sun.

Arise, fair sun, and kill the envious moon,

Who is already sick and pale with grief

That thou, her maid, art far more fair than she.

Be not her maid, since she is envious;

Her vestal livery is but sick and green,

And none but fools do wear it; cast it off.

It is my lady, O, it is my love!

O that she knew she were!

She speaks, yet she says nothing; what of that?

Her eye discourses, I will answer it.

I am too bold, 'tis not to me she speaks.

Two of the fairest stars in all the heaven,

Having some business, do entreat her eyes

To twinkle in their spheres till they return.

What if her eyes were there, they in her head?

—*Romeo & Juliet*: 2.2.2–18

And too soon marr'd are those so early made.

Earth hath swallowed all my hopes but she;

She's the hopeful lady of my earth.

But woo her, gentle Paris, get her heart,

My will to her consent is but a part;

And she agreed, within her scope of choice

Lies my consent and fair according voice.

This night I hold an old accustom'd feast,

Whereto I have invited many a guest,

Such as I love, and you, among the store

One more, most welcome, makes my number more.

At my poor house look to behold this night

Earth-treading stars that make dark heaven light.

—*Romeo & Juliet*: 1.2.13–25

You may light on a husband that hath no beard.

I have a good eye, uncle, I can see a church by daylight.

—*Much Ado About Nothing*: 2.1.13/24

I was about to tell thee—when my heart,

As wedged with a sigh, would rive in twain,

Lest Hector or my father should perceive me,

I have (as when the sun doth light a-scorn)

Buried this sigh in wrinkle of a smile,

But sorrow that is couch'd in seeming gladness

Is like that mirth fate turns to sudden sadness.

—*Troilus & Cressida*: 1.1.12

I am sick of this false world, and will love nought

But even the mere necessities upon't.

Then, Timon, presently prepare thy grave;

Lie where the light foam of the sea may beat

Thy grave-stone daily; make thine epitaph,

That death in me at others' lives may laugh.

—*Timon of Athens*: 4.3.331–336

Fair glass of light, I lov'd you, and could still,

Were not this glorious casket stor'd with ill.

But I must tell you, now my thoughts revolt,

For he's no man on whom perfections wait

That, knowing sin within, will touch the gate.

You are a fair viol, and your sense the strings;

Who, finger'd to make man his lawful music,

Would draw heaven down, and all the gods to hearken;

But being play'd upon before your time,

Hell only danceth at so harsh a chime.

Good sooth, I care not for you.

—*Pericles*: 1.1.76–86

A thousand times the worse, to want thy light.

Love goes toward love as schoolboys from their books,

But love from love, toward school with heavy looks.

—*Romeo & Juliet*: 2.2.155–157

Fie on sinful fantasy!

Fie on lust and luxury!

Lust is but a bloody fire,

Kindled with unchaste desire,

Fed in heart, whose flames aspire,

As thoughts do blow them, higher and higher.

Pinch him, fairies, mutually!

Pinch him for his villainy!

Pinch him, and burn him, and turn him about,

Till candles, and starlight, and moonshine be out.

—*Merry Wives of Windsor*: 5.5.67–76

O, were that all! I think not on my father,

And these great tears grace his remembrance more

Than those I shed for him. What was he like?

I have forgot him. My imagination

Carries no favor in't but Bertram's.

I am undone, there is no living, none,

If Bertram be away. 'Twere all one

That I should love a bright particular star

And think to wed it, he is so above me.

In this bright radiance and collateral light

Must I be comforted, not in his sphere.

Th' ambition in my love thus plagues itself:

The hind that would be mated by the lion

Must die for love. 'Twas pretty, though a plague,

To see him every hour, to sit and draw

His arched brows, his hawking eye, his curls,

In our heart's table—heart too capable

Of every line and trick of his sweet favor.

—*All's Well That Ends Well*: 1.1.40–57

When thou dost pinch thy bearer, thou dost sit

Like a rich armor worn in heat of day,

That scald'st with safety. By his gates of breath

There lies a downy feather which stirs not.

Did he suspire, that light and weightless down

Perforce must move. My gracious lord! My father!

This sleep is sound indeed, this is a sleep

That from this golden rigol hath divorc'd

So many English kings. Thy due from me

Is tears and heavy sorrows of the blood,

Which nature, love, and filial tenderness

Shall, O dear father, pay thee plenteously.

My due from thee is this imperial crown,

Which as immediate from thy place and blood,

Derives itself to me.

—*Henry IV, Part 2*: 4.5.28–42

Give me a torch, I am not for this ambling;

Being but heavy, I will bear the light.

—*Romeo & Juliet*: 1.4.11–12

Still do I see in him delineate

His mother's visage; those his eyes are hers,

Who, looking wistely on me, make me blush:

For faults against themselves give evidence;

Lust is fire, and men like lanterns show

Light lust within themselves, even through

themselves.

—*Edward III*: 2.2.87–92

Be kind and courteous to this gentleman,

Hop in his walks and gambol in his eyes;

Feed him with apricots and dewberries,

With purple grapes, green figs, and mulberries;

The honey-bags steal from the humble-bees,

And for night-tapers crop their waxen thighs,

And light them at the fiery glow-worm's eyes,

To have my love to bed and to arise;

And pluck the wings from painted butterflies,

To fan the moonbeams from his sleeping eyes.

Nod to him, elves, and do him courtesies.

—*A Midsummer Night's Dream*: 3.1.89–99

Good friend, go to him; for by this light of heaven,

I know not how I lost him. Here I kneel:

If e'er my will did trespass 'gainst his love,

Either in discourse of thought or actual deed,

Or that mine eyes, mine ears, or any sense

Delighted them in any other form;

Or that I do not yet, and ever did,

And ever will (though he do shake me off

To beggarly divorcement) love him dearly,

Comfort forswear me! Unkindness may do much,

And his unkindness may defeat my life,

But never taint my love.

—*Othello*: 4.2.150–161

My love (her mistress) is a gracious moon,

She (an attending star) scarce seen a light.

—*Love's Labour's Lost*: 4.3.205–206

How shall I dote on her with more advice,

That thus without advice begin to love her?

'Tis but her picture I have yet beheld,

And that hath dazzled my reason's light;

But when I look on her perfections,

There is no reason but I shall be blind.

If I can check my erring love, I will;

If not, to compass her I'll use my skill.

—*Two Gentlemen of Verona*: 2.4.194–201

Perchance light in the light.

I desire her name.

—*Love's Labour's Lost*: 2.1.194

Ask me no reason why I love you,

for though Love use Reason for his precisian,

he admits him not for his counsellor.

You are not young, no more am I;

go to then, there's sympathy. You are merry, so am I;

ha, ha! Then there's more sympathy.

You love sack, and so do I;

would you desire better sympathy?

Let it suffice thee, Mistress Page—at the least

if the love of a soldier can suffice—that I love thee.

I will not say, pity me—'tis not a soldier-like

phrase—but I say, love me. By me,

Thine own true knight,

By day or night,

Or any kind of light,

With all his might

For thee to fight . . .

—*Merry Wives of Windsor*: 2.1.2–5

Come, let us go. These things, come thus to light,

Smother her spirits up.

—*Much Ado About Nothing*: 4.1.102

Well, "set thee down, sorrow!"

for so they say the fool said, and so say I,

and I the fool: well prov'd, wit!

By the Lord, this love is as mad as Ajax. It kills sheep;

it kills me, I a sheep: well prov'd again a' my side!

I will not love; if I do, hang me; i' faith, I will not.

O but her eye—by this light, but for her eye,

I would not love her; yes, for her two eyes.

Well, I do nothing in the world but lie, and lie in my throat.

By heaven, I do love,

and it hath taught me to rhyme and to be melancholy;

and here is part of my rhyme, and here my melancholy.

Well, she hath one a' my sonnets already:

the clown bore it, the fool sent it, and the lady hath it:

sweet clown, sweeter fool, sweetest lady! By the world,

I would not care a pin, if the other three were in.

—*Love's Labour's Lost*: 4.3.1

Marry, so I mean, sweet Katherine, in thy bed;

And therefore setting all this chat aside,

Thus in plain terms: your father hath consented

That you shall be my wife; your dowry 'greed on;

And will you, nill you, I will marry you.

Now, Kate, I am a husband for your turn,

For by this light whereby I see thy beauty,

Thy beauty that doth make me like thee well,

Thou must be married to no man but me;

For I am he am born to tame you, Kate,

And bring you from a wild Kate to a Kate

Conformable as other household Kates.

—*Taming of the Shrew*: 2.1.258–269

Now God be prais'd, that to believing souls

Gives light in darkness, comfort in despair!

—*Henry VI, Part 2*: 2.1.65–66

True:

When the day serves, before black-corner'd night,

Find what thou want'st by free and offer'd light.

Come.

—*Timon of Athens*: 5.1.44–46

That light we see is burning in my hall.

How far that little candle throws his beams!

So shines a good deed in a naughty world.

—*The Merchant of Venice*: 5.1.86–88

Well, do not swear. Although I joy in thee,

I have no joy of this contract tonight,

It is too rash, too unadvis'd, too sudden,

Too like the lightning, which doth cease to be

Ere one can say it lightens. Sweet, good night!

This bud of love, by summer's ripening breath,

May prove a beauteous flow'r when next we meet.

Good night, good night! As sweet repose and rest

Come to thy heart as that within my breast!

—*Romeo & Juliet*: 2.2.116–124

Art thou come? Well, fellow,

I have hoped to save thine honesty a little.

Now, if thou canst give Wit any better council than I have done,

spare not. There I leave him to they mercy.

But by this time, I am sure, our banquet's ready:

My lord and ladies, we will taste that first,

And then they shall begin the play again,

Which through the fellow's absence, and by me,

Instead of helping, hath been hindered.

Prepare against we come. Lights there, I say!—

Thus fools oft times do help to mar the play.

—*Sir Thomas More*: 3.3.232–239

Go to, go to,

You are a saucy boy. Is't so indeed?

This trick may chance to scath you, I know what.

You must contrary me! Marry, 'tis time.—

Well said, my hearts!—You are a princox, go,

Be quiet, or—More light, more light!—For shame,

I'll make you quiet, what!—Cheerly, my hearts!

—*Romeo & Juliet*: 1.5.74–80

Within.

Give us a light there, ho!

A light, a light!

—*Macbeth*: 3.3.8/13

Through the house give glimmering light

By the dead and drowsy fire,

Every elf and fairy sprite

Hop as light as bird from brier,

And this ditty, after me,

Sing, and dance it trippingly.

—A Midsummer Night's Dream: 5.1.334–339

As little by such toys as may be possible:

Best sing it to the tune of "Light o' love."

—*Two Gentlemen of Verona*: 1.2.79–80

And so may you; for a light heart lives long.

—*Love's Labour's Lost*: 5.2.18

Clap 's into "Light a' love"; that goes without a burden.

Do you sing it, and I'll dance it.

—*Much Ado About Nothing*: 3.4.20

Come, come, we are friends.

Let's have a dance ere we are married, that we may

lighten our own hearts and our wives' heels.

—*Much Ado About Nothing*: 5.4.97

He'll dance the morris twenty mile an hour,

And that will founder the best hobby-horse

(If I have any skill) in all the parish,

And gallops to the tune of "Light a' love."

What think you of this horse?

—*Two Noble Kinsmen*: 5.2.51–55

Nay, stir there, fellows; fie, ye are too slow!

See that your lights be in a readiness:

The banquet shall be here. God's me, madame,

Leave my Lady Mayoress! Both of us from the board!

And my son Roper too! What may our guests think?

—*Sir Thomas More*: 3.3.15–19

Ay, sir, we did sleep day out of countenance,

and made the night light with drinking.

—*Antony & Cleopatra*: 2.2.171

More light, you knaves, and turn the tables up;

And quench the fire, the room is grown too hot.

Ah, sirrah, this unlook'd-for sport comes well.

Nay, sit, nay, sit, good cousin Capulet,

For you and I are past our dancing days.

How long is't now since last yourself and I

Were in a mask?

—*Romeo & Juliet*: 1.5.19–25

Give me some music. Now good morrow, friends.

Now, good Cesario, but that piece of song,

That old and antique song we heard last night;

Methought it did relieve my passion much,

More than light airs and recollected terms

Of these most brisk and giddy-paced times.

Come, but one verse.

—*Twelfth Night*: 2.4.1–6

Therefore, to be possess'd with double pomp,

To guard a title that was rich before,

To gild refined gold, to paint the lily,

To throw a perfume on the violet,

To smooth the ice, or add another hue

Unto the rainbow, or with taper-light . . .

—*King John*: 4.2.9–14

That's the way; for women are light at midnight.

—*Measure for Measure*: 5.1.266

To sing a song that old was sung,

From ashes ancient Gower is come,

Assuming man's infirmities,

To glad your ear and please your eyes.

It hath been sung at festivals,

On ember-eves and holy-ales;

And lords and ladies in their lives

Have read it for restoratives.

The purchase is to make men glorious,

Et bonum quo antiquius, eo melius.

If you, born in those latter times,

When wit's more ripe, accept my rhymes,

And that to hear an old man sing

May to your wishes pleasure bring,

I life would wish, and that I might

Waste it for you like taper-light.

—*Pericles*: 1-Prologue.1–16

Bear the lights close—where is the music, sirs?

—*Double Falsehood*: 1.3.1

"May you never more enjoy the light," etc.

Is not this a fine song?

—*Two Noble Kinsmen*: 4.1.105

How sweet the moonlight sleeps upon this bank!

Here will we sit, and let the sounds of music

Creep in our ears. Soft stillness and the night

Become the touches of sweet harmony.

Sit, Jessica. Look how the floor of heaven

Is thick inlaid with patens of bright gold.

There's not the smallest orb which thou behold'st

But in his motion like an angel sings,

Still quiring to the young-ey'd cherubins;

Such harmony is in immortal souls,

But whilst this muddy vesture of decay

Doth grossly close it in, we cannot hear it.

—*The Merchant of Venice*: 5.1.51–62

The crickets sing, and man's o'erlabor'd sense

Repairs itself by rest. Our Tarquin thus

Did softly press the rushes ere he waken'd

The chastity he wounded. Cytherea,

How bravely thou becom'st thy bed! Fresh lily,

And whiter than the sheets! That I might touch!

But kiss, one kiss! Rubies unparagon'd,

How dearly they do't! 'Tis her breathing that

Perfumes the chamber thus. The flame o' th' taper

Bows toward her, and would under-peep her lids,

To see th' enclosed lights, now canopied

Under these windows, white and azure lac'd

With blue of heaven's own tinct. But my design!

To note the chamber, I will write all down:

—*Cymbeline*: 2.2.11–23

A torch for me. Let wantons light of heart

Tickle the senseless rushes with their heels.

For I am proverb'd with a grandsire phrase,

I'll be a candle-holder and look on:

The game was ne'er so fair, and I am done.

—*Romeo & Juliet*: 1.4.35–39

This jest is dry to me. Gentle sweet,

Your wits makes wise things foolish. When we greet,

With eyes best seeing, heaven's fiery eye,

By light we lose light; your capacity

Is of that nature that to your huge store

Wise things seem foolish, and rich things but poor.

—*Love's Labour's Lost*: 5.2.373–378

Truly, and I hold ambition of so airy and light

a quality that it is but a shadow's shadow.

—*Hamlet*: 2.2.217

The fineness of which metal is not found

In fortune's love; for then the bold and coward,

The wise and fool, the artist and unread,

The hard and soft, seem all affin'd and kin;

But in the wind and tempest of her frown,

Distinction, with a broad and powerful fan,

Puffing at all, winnows the light away,

And what hath mass or matter, by itself

Lies rich in virtue and unmingled.

—*Troilus & Cressida*: 1.3.1

Believe me, I am passing light in spirit.

—*Henry IV, Part 2*: 4.2.85

Witness, you ever-burning lights above,

You elements that clip us round about,

Witness that here Iago doth give up

The execution of his wit, hands, heart,

To wrong'd Othello's service! Let him command,

And to obey shall be in me remorse,

What bloody business ever.

—*Othello*: 3.3.465

With love's light wings did I o'erperch these walls,

For stony limits cannot hold love out,

And what love can do, that dares love attempt;

Therefore thy kinsmen are no stop to me.

—*Romeo & Juliet*: 2.2.66–69

The law that threat'ned death becomes thy friend,

And turns it to exile: there art thou happy.

A pack of blessings light upon thy back,

Happiness courts thee in her best array,

But like a mishaved and sullen wench,

Thou pouts upon thy fortune and thy love.

Take heed, take heed, for such die miserable.

Go get thee to thy love as was decreed,

Ascend her chamber, hence and comfort her.

—*Romeo & Juliet*: 3.3.141–147

I should have been more strange, I must confess,

But that thou overheardst, ere I was ware,

My true-love passion; therefore pardon me,

And not impute this yielding to light love,

Which the dark night hath so discovered.

—*Romeo & Juliet*: 2.2.102–106

There is a kind of character in thy life,

That to th' observer doth thy history

Fully unfold. Thyself and thy belongings

Are not thine own so proper as to waste

Thyself upon thy virtues, they on thee.

Heaven doth with us as we with torches do,

Not light them for themselves; for if our virtues

Did not go forth of us, 'twere all alike

As if we had them not. Spirits are not finely touch'd

But to fine issues; nor Nature never lends

The smallest scruple of her excellence,

But like a thrifty goddess, she determines

Herself the glory of a creditor,

Both thanks and use. But I do bend my speech

To one that can my part in him advertise.

Hold therefore, Angelo:

In our remove be thou at full ourself.

—*Measure for Measure*: 1.1.27–43

For Imogen's dear life take mine, and though

'Tis not so dear, yet 'tis a life; you coin'd it.

'Tween man and man they weigh not every stamp;

Though light, take pieces for the figure's sake;

You rather, mine being yours; and so, great pow'rs,

If you will take this audit, take this life,

And cancel these cold bonds. O Imogen,

I'll speak to thee in silence.

—*Cymbeline*: 5.4.22–29

Sweet wife, good night, good night:

God send us all his everlasting light!

—*Sir Thomas More*: 5.3.126

Let all the number of the stars give light

To thy fair way.

—*Antony & Cleopatra*: 3.2.65

Stabs himself.

Thus die I, thus, thus, thus.

Now am I dead,

Now am I fled;

My soul is in the sky.

Tongue, lose thy light,

Moon, take thy flight,

Exit Moonshine.

Now die, die, die, die, die.

Dies.

—*A Midsummer Night's Dream*: 5.1.262–268

Tomorrow, and tomorrow, and tomorrow,

Creeps in this petty pace from day to day,

To the last syllable of recorded time;

And all our yesterdays have lighted fools

The way to dusty death. Out, out, brief candle!

Life's but a walking shadow, a poor player,

That struts and frets his hour upon the stage,

And then is heard no more. It is a tale

Told by an idiot, full of sound and fury,

Signifying nothing.

—*Macbeth*: 5.5.19–28

Why? All delights are vain, but that most vain

Which, with pain purchas'd, doth inherit pain:

As, painfully to pore upon a book

To seek the light of truth, while truth the while

Doth falsely blind the eyesight of his look.

Light, seeking light, doth light of light beguile;

So ere you find where light in darkness lies,

Your light grows dark by losing of your eyes.

—*Love's Labour's Lost*: 1.1.72–79

I am none, by this good light.

—*The Winter's Tale*: 2.3

APPENDIX

List of plays and number of passages cited from each.

ACKNOWLEDGMENTS

Tom Stoppard
Caitlin Murray
inspiration

PlayShakespeare.com
source text

Andres Pardo
research

Yolande McLean
editing

Chin-Yee Lai
cover design

Tisa Pro
typeface

www.ingramcontent.com/pod-product-compliance
Lightning Source LLC
Chambersburg PA
CBHW021842090426
42811CB00033B/2114/J